# TALES

## *from the*

# HILL

David R. Cox

PAGE PUBLISHING
Meadville, PA

First originally published by Page Publishing 2024

ISBN 979-8-88960-902-5 (pbk)
ISBN 979-8-88960-918-6 (digital)

Printed in the United States of America

# The Doughnut Adventure

When I was six years old, in between spoonfuls of Cap'n Crunch cereal and Saturday morning cartoons, I'd watch my brother Kenny iron his shirts and pants.

My mother long ago gave up offering to iron Ken's clothes; she would just neatly pile them on the big chair, and off he would go into production.

Clouds of steam billowed around him as he added more water to the large hot iron, working out every wrinkle.

Then, being careful to hang each shirt and a pair of pants properly in his closet.

He was sometimes more entertaining than the cartoons, only coming in second to watching him shave.

On this Saturday, he looked over at me, smiled, lifted a shirt from the ironing board, and asked, "Do you want to go downtown?"

I jumped out from under the coffee table and quickly put on my favorite shirt, pants, and Chuck Taylor sneakers.

I hugged my mom while she washed the kitchen windows.

Kenny threw my jacket over to me, and we headed for the back staircase.

The sun warmed us as we stepped off the back porch; it was going to be a great day.

Passing by Dartmouth Street School, I saw my friends playing Wiffle ball in the schoolyard.

They called me over to play, but I told them I was going downtown.

The bus stops in front of Joe's Spa.

Kenny's friends, Brian Foley and Jeff Hamilton, were standing in front of the spa; so we walked over.

These guys were some of the biggest pranksters I've ever met in my life.

My brother Steven and I never know what may show up in your bedroom from the night before.

It could be a rabbit in a cage or a stop sign with a metal pole and concrete post still attached to it.

I don't want to get into the Worcester airport landing light!

We all said, "Hi!" Brian and Kenny stepped aside to talk.

I looked up at Jeff; he smiled as only he could and asked, "Where are you going?"

I said, "Downtown."

Jeff kept smiling, reaching into his pocket. He handed me a ten-dollar bill and said, "Buy yourself something fun and memorable."

I saw the bus coming up the hill, and I thanked him while the bus rustled to a stop.

Kenny put his arm around my shoulder, then boosted me up into the bus.

I asked him what we were going to do downtown.

He replied, "We're going to Cottage Donuts."

That sounded good to me.

Getting closer to downtown, things began to change, with so many more cars and people.

The tall buildings looked so remarkable.

We got off the bus at the city hall, and Kenny caught me in midair, jumping off the bus onto the sidewalk.

I was ready to have some fun.

Walking along the sidewalk, our hands instinctively grasped.

I held on very tightly as I walked past the crowds of people rushing to their destinations.

Crossing Pleasant Street, I began to see the glass walls and bright neon signs spelling Cottage Donuts.

The smell of glazed chocolate doughnuts and warm coffee engulfed us as we walked in.

Kenny led me to a woman stacking coffee cups behind the glass counter, his friend Candace Jaegle.

She had a red bow holding back her long blond hair.

Finding the step under the counter, I boosted myself up onto the round leather-bound seat.

Kenny sat down and introduced us.

Candace said, "Hello," with a warm, ingratiating smile. "What can I get you?"

Looking at the display of doughnuts and pastries was overwhelming.

I decided on a chocolate-covered doughnut and chocolate milk.

Kenny seemed happy with a regular coffee and a plain doughnut.

Candace brought me the largest chocolate-covered doughnut I had ever seen.

It barely fit the white ceramic plate she put down on the counter.

She pulled back the cardboard cover from the chocolate milk bottle, poured it into a large glass, and handed me a straw. The doughnut and chocolate milk were delicious.

When we were finished, Kenny suggested I pick out a dozen doughnuts with Candace to bring home.

Candace smiled and started folding the sides of the doughnut box.

Picking out a dozen doughnuts must be one of life's great pleasures.

I started with my mom's favorite: two apricot jam-filled doughnuts.

Kenny finished up his coffee while Candace cut a piece of string from the rotating spool and tied it in a bow to tighten the box securely.

Kenny reached for his wallet. Looking up at him, I smiled, saying, "I got this," pulling the ten-dollar bill out of my pocket. I handed it over the glass counter to Candace.

Kenny looked down at me, trying not to look surprised, then started laughing, saying, "Leave a dollar."

Candace came around the counter with a warm smile and handed me the box of doughnuts.

I gave the dollar and change to Kenny and waited while they said goodbye.

We knew we would be kidding each other about this for a long time to come.

While crossing over the black-and-white tiled floor to leave, I could hear a little voice of wisdom saying, "Candace will be playing a very important part in your life."

I remember that day as one of my favorites.

# A Gardener's Story (Allen's Garden)

In my family, we grew up tending gardens.

We learned to pick weeds before we learned to walk.

I was raking the other day and started thinking about a story my brother-in-law Allen told me.

Allen is best described in good-hearted humor as "Jethro Bodine's evil twin."

He's the size of Jethro, just a little more eccentric in certain ways.

Allen is from Southern Alabama.

He and my sister met in Florida and decided to move to York, Maine.

Allen was having a tough time with the customs of Maine and the lack of real work available.

As all gardeners know that raising a garden can be very therapeutic.

Allen started a garden and used it as his refuge.

One day he came home from a dirty, sweaty construction job to find a neighbor poking around in his garden.

I can imagine the look on the guy's face when an angry six-foot-three-inch wild-haired Southern "boy" comes standing over him and says, "Don't fuck with my therapy."

The guy probably dropped some "fertilizer" in his pants and ran.

This story still makes me laugh.

# Mrs. Virginia (Gennie) George

I recently opened some storage boxes and found a gift (a crystal apple).

A wonderful elderly Syrian woman had given it to me.

Her name was Virginia (Gennie) George.

She would call me for help doing yard work.

My "second" favorite day with her was while gathering up pears that had fallen from the tree in the backyard, I looked up to see her sitting on the lawn, hand-cutting with scissors every blade of grass around the flagstone walks.

Her patience and serenity were incredible.

My "first" favorite time with her was when she called me to trim the hedges at her home.

I started up the hedge trimmer and brought them down well enough. I began to trim the sides.

From behind me, I could hear the sliding glass door opening, and I could see Mrs. George walking over to me in her housecoat and sneakers, motioning to cut shorter, shorter.

Wiping her hands, she went back into her house.

I continued cutting and gathering more clippings than I anticipated.

Her street was a dead end with a park on one side and a railroad embankment on the other.

I decided to spread the clippings in the back of the park.

But the postal worker, having lunch down there, didn't take too kindly to my actions.

I was loading up my truck again when a police car parked up at the end of the driveway.

He began to question me about what was going on.

From behind, I could hear the sliding glass door opening.

A smile came to my face.

Mrs. George (all five feet four inches of her) came out in her housecoat and slippers.

She said, "Hello," to the officer and asked his name.

He replied, "Officer Coleman."

She said, "Oh, weren't you here last week visiting my husband with Captain Sean O'Malley and Lieutenant Bill Sullivan?"

You see, Gennie's husband and two sons have been constables in Worcester County for over forty-five years.

The patrol officer looked around me. The look on his face said it all; these were two ranking officers he didn't want to answer to.

He looked around at the clippings, then down at her, and said, "I understand the situation, ma'am. Have a nice day."

He turned around, said nothing to me, and got in his cruiser.

Gennie looked up at me, winked, and went back into the house.

I'm very honored; this is the gift she chose to give me upon her passing.

Seeing it, I'm able to be reminded of her patience, serenity, and sense of humor in life.

# Dr. Jankowski at Sea

One spring morning, my neighbor, Dr. Thaddeus Jankowski, called me, asking if I would help him till his garden.

Dr. Jankowski was a dentist of Polish descent and a retired lieutenant commander in the US Navy.

I knew from past experiences that there would be no rototiller involved, the soil would be turned over by hand with a pitchfork and rakes.

Hard work was the only way a man of his generation knew how to do things.

Because of the respect I had for him and his wife, I would never refuse any request.

And I knew he would have another great story to tell as we worked.

We started turning the soil and pulling weeds.

Dr. J told me a story about serving on a hospital ship in the Pacific.

The captain required all officers to wear their sidearms while attending morning reveille.

He stopped digging, looked at me, and said, "I'm a man who alleviates pain. I'm not about to cause it."

He didn't wear his sidearm during the first-morning reveille.

The captain cited him for this.

He decided it was better to wear the sidearm than get reprimanded.

He started to laugh and said, "That is, until word came down that the captain had broken a tooth and was requesting an immediate appointment."

He looked around at all the patients already waiting, but he shook his head, agreeing to the captain's request.

After the procedure, the captain and the doctor agreed that he wouldn't have to wear his sidearm again at reveille.

That was the day of the dedication of the new Korean War memorial downtown.

His wife called him from the back door, reminding him that it was time to get ready for the ceremony.

We finished digging, and the doctor went inside to change.

I put the tools away in the shed and washed my face in the utility sink.

We had gotten especially dirty that day.

Closing the sled door, I noticed Mrs. Jankowski bring out a large glass of lemonade with a generous smile. She thanked me while handing me a fifty-dollar check.

I put the check in my pocket, knowing it was useless to refuse.

I sat in the shade under the grapevine trestle, finishing my glass of lemonade.

About a half-hour later, the doctor came out of the back door of his house.

He was dressed in a pristinely conditioned naval uniform; not a speck of lint was on him.

Every hair was in place.

My jaw dropped at the change in his appearance.

He sat down in the passenger seat of their Lincoln Town Car.

Mrs. Jankowski put on her sunglasses, waved, and backed out of their driveway.

The doctor gazed out the window, immersed in his thoughts.

Dr. Jankowski is one of the greatest humanitarians I've ever known.

# The Ghost of Red Cox

"I've been coming to this bar since I was a kid," said Will, the bearded, heavily tattooed ironworker, to Sonia, a sleek, immaculately dressed Asian businesswoman, who happened to be in his neighborhood bar, the 7-11, where there is always good conversation and everyone is welcome.

Sonia smiled, placing her eyeglasses on the bar. She shook out her hair and began to relax while she and Will shared a deeply flavorful bottle of merlot.

Will continued, "My father used to work across the street for a liquor distributor called Premium Beverage. On hot summer nights, he'd stop here for a few drafts."

Will laughed. "No, there wasn't just one or two beers for my dad. He was a hard drinker, my father. But in those days, you could get away with it, and get away with it he did. He loved drinking draft beer.

"My mother would send the next available kid down the hill to get him. When it was my turn, I'd walk through the open wooden front door, and there he would be, sitting up strong at the bar in his Premium Beverages uniform and his name 'Ralph' sewn on his shirt.

"Everyone knows him as Red for his thick red hair parted in the middle. He wasn't a loud guy, just very sociable, and had a viable interest in the outcome of sporting events," Will said with a wink.

Sonia laughed as only a gambler would understand.

"He'd be happy to see me hand me a handful of quarters and buy me a Coke. I'd wait by the jukebox and play my favorite songs because he did have one rule, 'Never leave the bar till you've finished your drink.'"

Kim, the waitress, stirred the straw as she brought me over a delicious-looking Coke with crushed ice and lime. She knows how much I really like it.

I waited while he and his friend Bill Miley reminisced about the time Red's truck broke down in the small town of Hudson.

The young tow truck operator started lifting the truck when Red asked if they could tow the truck down the street to make a delivery.

The tow truck driver lifted the truck and carried it down the street.

The operator pulled up to the loading dock and began to help unload the cases of beer.

The tow truck driver looked out from the loading dock as Red handed the bartender the delivery slip to sigh.

The bartender handed Red back the book of slips and two cold beers, handing one of the beers to the tow truck operator. He asked, "Does this happen often?"

Red's reply was "It's customary."

The operator smiled and said, "Let's tow the truck throughout the town, finish your deliveries, then we'll bring it back to Worcester."

They both had a hearty laugh.

"While listening to the songs on the jukebox, I would see Jake, 'the local bookie,' and his walrus-sized friend Phil sitting at a table in the back. Jake would look me in the eye, hold a glance, and smile. We had long passed the conversations of him describing what an incredible high school football player my father was. Often describing the speed, my father had to catch a Hail Mary pass or the ferocious blocks he would make to stop the opponent. He'd often tell me that if he had stayed with it, he would probably be coaching an NFL team."

Sonia looked over at the jukebox and asked, "Is that the same one?"

Will laughed and said, "Yes, it is," taking a sip of his wine. "Still works great."

Sonia continued to look around the vintage bar.

She admired the hardwood wainscoting surrounding the rectangular walls, the copper ceiling, and the different decades of local sports team photographs on the walls. She marveled at the long hand-carved bar and the beveled glass. The bar was a work of art. Sonia felt a kind warmth in the air as she watched the people in the neighborhood share stories and have drinks. Will gestured to see if Sonia would like more wine. Sonia smiled and raised her glass forward under Will's massive arm.

Will continued the conversation.

"I was walking my Lab, Cedar, in Falmouth, Massachusetts, last summer, when I saw a man raking his yard wearing a Teamsters Local 170 sweatshirt. That was my father's labor union in Worcester. When I came over to introduce myself, he stopped raking to pat Cedar, which turned into a tail-wagging festival.

"I asked him about his Local 170 sweatshirt. He said he had been a member for over thirty years and now sat on the retirement board. I asked him if he ever worked with Red Cox."

Sonia paused while Will spoke about his father.

"The neighbor's eyes widened, his jaw dropped slightly, and he stepped back as if a strong breeze had just hit him. I don't think he ever expected to hear that name again. He laughed and said, 'Sure, I did. Is that your father?' 'Yes,' I replied.

"He looked me straight in the eye and said, 'Working with your father were the hardest days I ever worked in my life. I made good money, but I worked my ass off. Yeah, we'd sit in the cab, and he would go through the day's delivery slips.'

"He began to imitate my father, saying, 'Ya, we'll get a drink [a beer] from this guy. Er, we'll be lucky to get a glass of water from this bastard.'

"The neighbor went on, 'By eleven in the morning, we'd already drank eight beers and delivered 183 cases of liqueur. I nearly passed out in the passenger seat. Red looked over at me and said, "Are you alright, kid?"'"

"The man leaned on his rake and said, 'I took over driving his truck when he retired. He gave me a bit of advice before handing me the keys. He said to do the job like the guy who must come back to fix the mistake.'

"It was wonderful to hear my father's voice again," Will said.

Just then, a late summer breeze quickly blew from the open back through the front doors of the bar, creating a wonderful chill throughout.

The band began to warm up.

Will began to applaud the band enthusiastically.

Sonia looked up at Christian, the bartender, as she began lighting candles at dusk.

They both smiled.

Sonia continued to smile, putting her hand on Will's tree-trunk thigh, knowing there would be more wine and good times ahead.

# The El Morocco Restaurant

A rite of passage for high schoolers on Grafton Hill was to work at the El Morocco Restaurant at 100 Wall Street, run by the eight children of Paul and Helen Aboody.

In 1943, the Aboodys opened a Middle Eastern restaurant at 73 Wall Street in a converted triple-decker.

The word spread throughout Boston and New England of this unique restaurant. The El became the place to go after hours to eat, drink, and party until 5:00 a.m.

Many famous people performing in the area would come to eat great food and meet the Aboodys as hosts, leaving many autographed photos and immemorial good times in the small restaurant.

In December 1977, the family opened the two-hundred-seat dining room and nightclub across the street from the original restaurant, looking over the city.

It opened to a crowd of five thousand people.

It was a step above any other restaurant in the area.

From sitting in a booth looking up at marvelous framed autograph photos to dancing in the Nile lounge all night, it was like stepping into Las Vegas on Grafton Hill.

As a busboy, I learned the fine art of balancing a tray full of dishes throughout a crowded restaurant while wearing a tuxedo shirt, bowtie, pants, and cummerbund.

All this time you are trying to keep up with the Aboodys' energy level and how efficiently they run their restaurant serving hundreds of meals on a weekend.

The restaurant always anticipated a celebrity would show up.

Part of the restaurant's excitement was not knowing who would be arriving for dinner that night—from Bette Midler dancing to the beat of Middle Eastern music to Rodney Dangerfield who described the restaurant by saying, "A great view, if only there was a view."

On one Saturday night, word spread in the kitchen of Worcester's own precarious son Abbie Hoffman was in the crowd of three hundred people attending a local college football banquet.

Abbie was just beginning to resurface at the time.

That night I made it my mission to spot him in the large crowd. When I did, he laughed having spotted me twenty minutes before.

Later in the kitchen, he gave an autograph saying, "Take it easy, Dave, but take it."

After the Saturday night crowd would head for the doors, the Aboodys would be heading to breakfast till 5:00 a.m. with whoever else wanted to go. Usually, a crowd of about twenty people would join them at the breakfast and tell old stories.

When I finally woke up late on Sunday afternoon, I'd reached into my purple-and-gold velvet Crown Royal bag to find at least a couple hundred dollars of tips inside.

It was a very exciting time.

The restaurant has since closed and was demolished in March 2016.

But as fate would have it, my sister Nancy brought home one of the many weeping fig trees that were in pots throughout the restaurant.

This small tree wasn't doing well. After spending some time with it, she got it to bloom again.

It never made it back to the restaurant and has been enjoying the sunshine by my living room window for the last thirty years. It is the last living object of a once great restaurant.

On July 31, 2023, the portion of 100 Wall Street was honorarily changed to Aboody Way.

# My Three Amigos

I once heard it said, "You're living a good life if you have one good friend."

You can call at any time.

I'm very fortunate I have three.

My friends are Sunderland (Sunny for short), Tony, and Billy (Bones) Bragg.

## My friend Sunny

My "go-to" drinking buddy is my neighborhood friend Sunderland or Sunny for short.

Sunny rides a Harley in almost any weather.

He is a wonderful combination of Keith Moon, Billy Joel, and Freddy Mercury.

I think there is a little cat in the mix, too, because he does have nine lives.

As was the case, when he was driving a friend around in a convertible Triumph TR-6, probably blasting George Michael's "Freedom," rounding a corner at some rate of speed, they swerved off the road through a cornfield, barely navigating the car through the center of two large Oak trees.

Stocks and stocks of corn fell into the convertible's backseat.

Sunny finally got the car to stop about fifty feet in, surrounded by corn.

They got out, looked at each other, then looked over at the car.

It had minor damage but no flat tires. They backed the TR-6 out as quickly as possible.

They shucked and ate corn all weekend; glad to be alive.

Sunny has a better sense of humor and emotional intelligence than anyone I know for bringing people together.

Fair warning: upon meeting someone new, Sunny will introduce you as a Harvard University psychology professor or whatever doctorate degree he thinks up at that time and walk away, leaving you and the other person smiling with drinks in your hands with the other person saying, "Really? Now with your newly appointed doctorate from the School of Hard Knocks?" You can bullshit the other person for as long as you want.

This is one of my favorite stories of all time.

In the mid-'80s, he and a friend decided to go fishing while driving around Cape Cod in a VW Bug.

Oh, did I fail to mention they did mescaline along the way?

They had a great day fishing, and as it got dark, they made a wrong turn onto Marchant Avenue in Hyannis Port and slowly approached the Kennedy compound, at a time when the Kennedys were still in high political office.

Sunny liked the view of the ocean and wanted to continue fishing.

He started to get out of the car.

The Secret Service agents with the Uzis tucked under their baggy polo shirts protecting the compound just smiled and shook their heads.

They led them back down the road to the VW Bug and watched them go on their way.

Sunny makes me laugh the hardest of anyone I know, and sometimes all you need in life is a friend who can make you laugh.

## *My friend Tony*

In Tony's world, there are three prices: wholesale, retail, and Tony's price.

Tony is so cheap on a Saturday night that he would rip the cologne samples out of men's magazines and rub them on his chest to go out.

He's the original to go through the McDonald's drive-up window and ask for extra ketchup to refill his bottle at home.

I had to convince him there wasn't a clearance section at the Dollar Store.

One winter, he called me to come over to his house.

A department store was running a promotion, handing out discount scratch-off coupons.

Tony got ahold of some 75 percent off coupons, this being around Christmas. And since I was the friend with the truck, we headed to the department store, grabbed a couple of carts like a couple of "bad Santas," and made our way to the electronics aisle, first grabbing a big-screen TV for us to watch football games (there are priorities) then several electronic gifts for his kids (he had four at the time). When we got our fill, we headed to the checkout lines.

The cashier handed him some more discount coupons, and with a slide of hand, Tony handed her back the 75 percent off coupons.

"Boy." She looked at him, so surprised. "Look," she said, "you got 75 percent off the purchase."

He looked at me with a "no shit" expression and tried to look surprised at her.

He started unloading the TV and other gifts.

I could only bite my lip from bursting out laughing, but he saved over four hundred dollars.

I have all sorts of wholesale, retail, and Tony's-price stories.

But for all his thriftiness, he spends very generously on his family at home and friends.

He is an incredible chef who has hosted many memorable parties.

## *Bill (Bones) Bragg*

I worked for over thirty years alongside Bill Bragg as a land surveyor.

From the grounds of prestigious colleges to the sloppiest mud-hole construction sites in ten-degree weather.

We learned to laugh at all the situations we found ourselves in.

We had a working connection and trust in our working abilities and each other.

We were often called upon to help complete several incredible building projects.

Bill is a true Irishman, smart as a whip, and can do trigonometric calculations in his head while drinking vodka with a cloud of cigarette smoke circling him.

The first week I met Bill, I wasn't sure what he looked like; there was so much cigarette smoke around him.

He could party all night and still come to work and do the job better than anyone else you could ever see.

He is simply indestructible.

Bill's mom, Peggy, was a truly delightful woman.

She would take the bus downtown just to sit in Worcester Common.

We would often see her there just enjoying the sunny day.

When circumstances became especially challenging at work for Bill and me, we would look at each other and quote Peggy, "It's a great life if you don't weaken."

In a sense, if she could do it, there's nothing to stop us from doing whatever we needed to do.

Peggy, the avid wrestling fan, had a subscription to *WWF Magazine*, which came once a month.

It was the highlight of Bill's day—to bring her mail in with the latest wrestling magazine for her.

Our work was often out of town, staying in hotel rooms.

(Please note: all the stories are true.)

## *In Northampton, Massachusetts*

We once worked a ten-hour day in Northampton, then checked into the local hotel for the night.

Standing behind the desk was Mark.

Mark was a skinny guy with a skinny body, a skinny tie, and skinny pants.

In his skinny voice, he said to Bill, "Please sign in confirming you requested a smoking room and that you won't be bringing any animals into the room with you."

We looked at each other about the animal part as he began to sign the papers.

Next, it was my turn to confirm that I had requested a non-smoking room and that I would not bring any animals into the room.

I leaned over the desk, and from behind, I heard Bill say out loud, "Does this mean we have to leave the sheep in the van?"

Bill has dentures but never wears them. I'm sure his toothless grin made an even bigger impact on Mark.

Bill doesn't have much of a filter on what he says or does; he just doesn't have to give a fuck.

I just gazed up and smiled.

Poor Mark really didn't know what to say.

That night, Bill decided to take the work truck and go buy a pack of cigarettes.

It was a warm night, and I was sitting outside my room when I saw the truck limping along the side of the road; it seemed to have no power to climb the hill.

I watched as the guy behind Bill kept blasting his horn at him.

Bill pulled into the motel parking lot in front of me and got out while the other guy pulled to the side of the road.

"Yeah, the damn truck lost power coming up the hill," he said, and this dick is yelling at me, "You're going too slow."

We looked over to the guy at the side of the road, and he was yelling, "You're glowing, you're glowing," pointing to the underside of the truck.

We looked below to see the catalytic converter glowing white hot next to the fuel tank.

The guy hurried away, thinking the truck was going to blow up.

Bill and I went into his room and grabbed a beer. I could only laugh, thinking this guy can even survive a "car bomb."

## Williamstown, Massachusetts

We went out to Williamstown, Massachusetts, to do work for Williams College.

My wife decided to have a little fun and packed a teddy bear in my suitcase.

That time Bill and I shared a room; and surprise, when I opened the suitcase, there it was. There was no hiding it.

I laughed, but Bill didn't have any of it.

I came out of the bathroom, and the teddy bear was hanging from the curtain rod.

So I left it there. It added a real attraction to the room.

The only thing was the next day when we came back from work.

The two wonderful gay owners of the hotel came walking over to us with the teddy bear in their hands.

A little girl had left hers behind. When they tried to look for it.

Lo and behold, they saw "Teddy" hanging from the curtain rod in our room.

They were a little confused.

Worse was trying to explain to them that it was *mine*.

## On Cape Cod

We went down to Cape Cod to work in the offseason.

They put us up in a really nice hotel.

Bill went out on the deck of his room to have a quick smoke.

He shut the glass door behind him, not realizing it would lock him outside.

Now there he was standing on a desolate Cape Cod hotel deck, locked out of his room with no cell phone and, worse for him, no more cigarettes as it started to get cold and dark.

So what did he decide to do? He saw a large bush below and decided to jump twenty feet into it, hoping it would break his fall.

I was sitting in my room, finishing my third beer by the warm fireplace, when the phone rang.

It's Bill saying you are not going to believe what happened to me.

Besides a couple of scratches, he was fine.

Still truly indestructible.

## *Bill the Golfer*

This may sound offensive, but remember, this is all true.

We were working at UMass Amherst when a double amputee walked out of a building with a Titlist golf hat on. I didn't think too much of it and just said, "Hi."

Bill and I were about three hundred feet away as I watched the guy walk by him.

Bill said something to him, and the guy seemed to stop in shock, then kept walking.

I walked back to Bill. I knew this wasn't going to be good.

I asked him what he said to the guy. Well, he said, "I saw his Titlist hat and asked him what his handicap was."

(Sorry, it's too funny not to tell.)

One of our jobs was a topographic survey of a twenty-acre abandoned drive-in theater.

As we got closer to the woods, we started to see golf balls lying there.

Come to find out the drive-in theater boarded a country club.

Bill is an avid golfer. We started each morning with a shopping bag and gathered an endless supply of practice balls for Bill.

For me, it was like an Easter egg hunt, seeing a little glimmer of a ball in the dirt and pulling it out. It was fun. We had two shopping bags full in a few hours.

A nice dog showed up as we started looking for more golf balls closer and closer to the country club, which was nice until the dog ran over the golf course while the golfers were teeing off.

Bill and I stayed still in the woods, watching the golfers chase the dog away.

We figured we'd better quit now.

Back at our work truck, we had plenty of golf balls to drive.

We came back from lunch. I was headed toward the woods when I heard, "Look out!" Bill had driven a ball with its course heading right for my head.

I turned around to see a white sphere heading right for me.

To this day, I can still remember the sound of it buzzing by my head as I ducked.

The look on Bill's face from three hundred feet away was priceless.

Some of the most fun we had was playing practical jokes on ourselves or any victim who came around.

We used walkie-talkies to communicate on the job.

I had my walkie-talkie on while I was "standing" in a men's room when I started hearing Prince's song "Purple Rain" come over a walkie-talkie speaker.

Being "incapacitated" at the time, all I could do was let the song continue to play, getting some very strange looks from the other guys as they zipped up their flies and tried to get away from me as fast as they could.

You would think I'd learn my lesson, but no.

A few months later, I walked into an office building to inform the receptionist we would be working outside.

As soon as she looked up to say, "May I help you?" I heard over the walkie-talkie, "I want a damn coke."

I turned around to see him through the window with his "shit-eating grin" and a toothless smile, giggling at me.

She was ready to call security. I said, "You'll have to excuse him. Tourette's."

Bill has a daughter, Jenn.

As a young girl, Jenn wrote her father a note to stop smoking cigarettes so he would be around for her first child.

Bill showed me the note one cold rainy morning.

In a cloud of cigarette smoke, he said, "How am I going to fulfill this?"

Some time has passed. Bill retired and stopped smoking.

He is the proud grandfather of two grandsons, Mason and Cameron.

And he is still indestructible.

I'm very grateful to continue these friendships with all my neighbors from Grafton Hill.

# Sitto

## A Short Story

John Taylor dribbled his basketball along the sidewalk to the court in the park.

Being the captain of his team, he always warms up early.

He was thinking about the assault and robbery of the young woman he and his friend Billy had witnessed.

They were placed in police custody and relied upon to make a positive identification of the attacker, Joe Collins, who was sent to prison for five years.

He was glad that it was over, or so he thought.

Turning the corner into the large tree-lined park, John dribbled faster, passing people left and right, excited to play basketball again.

As he was walking through the gate of the twelve-foot-high chain-link fence, he stepped onto the raised asphalt of the basketball court, which sent a rush of adrenaline through him. He dashed the length of the court; he was bouncing up for his first dunk of the season and was hanging on the rim long enough to see his girlfriend Susan sitting on the home team's bleachers, talking with her friends.

During the middle of practice, he noticed a group of boys about his age wearing red headbands and dew rags around their necks staring at him through all sides of the fence while he moved up and down the court.

He was getting a bad feeling about this.

When practice ended, Susan came down to the fence gate; she gave John a cold bottle of water and smiled. Glossing her lips, she said, "My mom is working a double shift. Do you want to come over?"

John sipped the water slowly, looking around at the kids with red headbands and dew rags now sitting on the visitor bleachers, smoking cigarettes.

The tallest of them kept staring at him, exhaling smoke in a large cloud.

John said, "Not today. I've got some things to do."

John sensed trouble; it was best not to get Susan involved.

She looked at him, very disappointed.

John gave her a hug and sent her back to sit with her girlfriends.

As he left the park, the group of kids started to follow him.

Quickly coming up from behind, they surrounded him, leading him into an alley.

Pushing him back and forth between them, they finally knocked him to the ground.

The tallest one hovered over him, blowing smoke in his face, then took the cigarette out of his mouth and flicked it at John.

John began to get very scared but refused to show it.

The thug put his foot on John's chest and spoke. "So you're the one who squealed on my brother."

John said, "I had no choice."

The thug started to laugh, pressing his foot harder into John's chest. He said, "Well, you know, I have no choice but to make your life miserable till he gets out of jail." The rest of the gang started to laugh. The thug looked down at John's sneakers. "Take them off."

John hesitated.

The thug pressed even harder on his chest and said, "Now!"

He stepped on John with all his weight.

John sat up, took off his sneakers, and handed them to him.

The thug tied the laces together and tossed them over a telephone wire.

They went up so far that John could not possibly get them down.

The group started to laugh even louder. John continued to sit on the pavement.

The thug looked down at John again, saying. "This is just the start of your problems. You should have kept your mouth shut, you little fink. That goes for your friend too. He'll be getting the same when I see him."

He and the gang started walking away. Then the young thug turned back to John and said, "It was nice to meet you. Looking forward to seeing you again really soon."

The whole gang looked back and started to laugh at John for continuing to sit on the pavement.

John wanted to cry, but he wouldn't let these punks get the best of him.

He took his socks off and started walking home barefoot.

John came home to find his grandmother clipping out a recipe from the newspaper in the kitchen.

He slipped into the bathroom past her, brushing his hair back and looking up into the mirror, feeling very alone.

He doesn't like to keep things from his grandmother, but he also doesn't like to make her worry.

He knew he would have to fight Joe Collins's brother to end this.

He looked down at his bare feet. Losing his new basketball shoes made him the angriest.

John's grandmother called for him loudly.

He tried to stay behind her in the kitchen.

She pointed to an envelope on the table and asked him to bring it down to Sitto as she walked around the kitchen, gathering ingredients for the recipe she found.

Sitto owns the house they live in; she is an elder Lebanese woman whose house is full of antiques and always smells like roses.

She always wears long black dresses, stockings, and black shoes with her long hair tied back into a tight bun. She does not speak very much English, so John and she only communicate through gestures.

She always offers him a plate full of homemade cookies to sit down and enjoy before he leaves.

John put on some old, tattered sneakers as he walked down the back staircase, still very upset.

He tried to swallow it while knocking on Sitto's door.

Sitto opened the door wide; her brilliant blue eyes looked at him with great concern as he walked into the house.

John handed her the envelope; she put it in a table drawer in the hallway, then motioned him into the kitchen.

John sat down, placing his hands on the linen tablecloth draped over the long wooden table overlooking her garden.

Sitto went into the small bathroom off the kitchen, rinsing out a face cloth with cold water.

She gently washed John's face, drying it with a soft towel, and smiled. Her pearl-white smile was illuminating.

She doesn't smile too often, and it brought great joy to John, but he could not forget what had happened.

She poured him a glass of cold milk and opened the antique metal box she where kept her cookies.

Patting John on the back, she walked slowly over to the stove to stir the soup she was making. Then she turned to look at John's bruises and dirty torn shirt.

John sat quietly, looking out the window. The cookies and cold milk tasted very good.

Feeling full, he got up from the table and began to leave.

Sitto walked him to the back door.

She paused before he left, put her hand on his cheek, and looked over at a religious statue, then looked up at him. Her hand became very warm. She smiled and opened the door; they both waved goodbye.

As the door closed, John walked up the heavy wooden steps to his grandmother's apartment.

Sitto walked back to the kitchen, opening a drawer under the telephone.

She opened her address book and began to slowly dial the phone.

Later that day, she slowly and peacefully walked to the neighborhood park.

Sitting on a wooden bench, she fed the squirrels and chipmunks scurrying at her feet.

From a distance, a tall, extremely muscular man full of tattoos walked toward her.

His hair was long and thick, a deep shade of black with strands of gray flowing through it.

His face was very tight and clean-shaven. He wore a black tank top and a denim jacket with the sleeves cut off, accentuating his muscles.

The buttons of the jacket were stamped with skulls and crossbones.

Black jeans ran the length of his long legs down to his black motorcycle boots.

He took his large rings off his hands as he approached her.

Sitto looked up at him. Her face brightened, and she extended her hand, saying, "Paul."

He cupped her hand in his, giving her his warmth.

He gently asked this grandmother in Lebanese, "What is troubling you?"

She looked up at him with great concern, explaining how bruised John appeared.

She did not want harm to escalate any further for him, especially while he was living inside her home.

She reached into her coat pocket and dropped a nut for the chipmunk sitting beneath the bench.

Paul didn't take his gaze away from her, assuring her that he would look into it and asking, "Where can I find John?"

Sitto told him he would be working the weekends at Mr. Billing's hardware store.

Paul gently smiled at her and squeezed her hand, then looked over to another man wearing motorcycle leather standing by a tree.

He motioned him over.

The man walked over to the right side of Sitto and carefully watched her push herself off the bench. Standing between the two men, she took their arms and began to walk, exhaling deeply and faintly.

The men walk her over to a running town car with tinted windows.

They guided her into the air-conditioned backseat.

Buckling her seatbelt, they softly closed the car door.

The car slowly left the curb.

A few days later, John heard the bells on the inside door handle of the hardware store begin to ring.

He turned to see two men with dark sunglasses walking through the door.

They looked like they belonged on the state prison football team.

Paul closed the door.

On his hands, he was wearing his large rings through fingerless gloves.

His companion looked like a Samoan wrestler. He weighed more than three hundred pounds with a bald head and long braided goatee with many tattoos and piercings. The large ring through his nose gave him the appearance of a raging bull.

He had walked with his hands in the pockets of a tightly buttoned leather trench coat.

The men came closer to him.

John thought, *Great, now the thug sent his father to beat me up*.

Paul looked down at John, paused, and said, "Are you John Taylor?"

John nodded his head.

Paul said, "I understand you were pushed around by some punks."

Paul asked how many there were.

"About six," John said.

Paul looked down at John's tattered sneakers. Taking off his sunglasses, he said, "My name is Paul, and I bet you'd like to get some revenge on them and a new pair of sneakers."

Mr. Billings opened the cellar door.

The two men turned quickly and stared at him.

Mr. Billings looked back in fear.

John said to him, "These men are friends of mine."

Mr. Billings looked at him strangely.

Paul turned to Mr. Billings, saying, "That's right. We were about to take John to lunch."

Mr. Billings looked down at his watch. It was 10:45 a.m. when he looked up.

John and the men headed through the door.

Outside, he saw another man sitting on a motorcycle beside two other motorcycles.

Paul walked over to the man sitting outside and began to talk.

The raging bull walked John over to his motorcycle, handed him a helmet, and straddled his motorcycle upright, kickstarting it to a loud roar. John climbed on the back.

He noticed on the back of Paul's coat a large *V* with the word *Vigilantes* embossed above it. The letters *MC* were under the *V*.

John looked at the front of Paul's jacket. It said, "President."

The raging bull had "Sergeant at Arms" on the front of his jacket.

Paul finished talking with the other biker. Walking over to his motorcycle, he tightened his greased-stained fingerless gloves around the throttle of his motorcycle. Placing some chewing tobacco between his teeth and cheeks, he kickstarted the bike alive to a thunderous roar.

After revving up the throttles, the three men roared down the street.

The Bull told John to hang on.

John began to think he was in a strange movie.

He had a feeling this was going to be one heck of a ride.

John shouted, "How do you know where they are?"

The Bull laughed and said, "Rats never go far from their holes."

They rode over to the alley where the boys had attacked John.

Paul and the raging bull roared up the alley.

The echo of the motorcycle's exhaust made the approach even more menacing.

The group of young thugs was standing in a doorway halfway up the alley.

John looked up to see the third biker blocking the other end of the alley.

Paul got off his bike and tightened up his fingerless gloves and large rings. He walked over to the whole gang of thugs while the Bull reached inside his trench coat.

Not knowing what he may have inside his coat, none of the thugs moved.

Paul looked at John, then quickly back at the group of thugs.

He grabbed the first one that made eye contact with John.

It was the tallest one. Paul grabbed him hard, pulled him away from the rest of the group, and spit a wad of tobacco at his feet.

"So you think you're badass," Paul said, showing no pity for his young age.

The raging bull continued to stare at the rest of the gang.

Paul said, "What's your name, boy?"

The thug still tried to act like he was tough and snickered. "People call me Spider."

Paul put his arm around the young thug's shoulder and spit another large wad of tobacco at his foot and said, "I don't like spiders. I usually squish them with my boot." He raised the sharp edge of his heavy motorcycle boot.

Paul said, "Listen to me carefully. It has come to my attention that you have threatened my friend John here."

The thug didn't say anything. He just stared forward.

Paul grabbed the thug and picked him up off the ground by his neck, shooting daggers at him with his eyes, saying, "If you are making a threat toward him, you are making a threat toward me. Is that something you want to do?"

Paul continued staring at him with fiery eyes.

The thug looked at Paul. The front of his pants began to get wet. He said, "No, I don't want any problems with you."

Paul lowered him to the ground, throwing him back into the gang.

The thug brushed himself off and said, "Who are you guys?"

Paul looked back at him and said, "We're John's guardian angels."

The Bull started to laugh under his breath.

With a roar, Paul said, "If any one of you comes fifty feet near John or any of his friends, I won't be so nice the next time. Do I make myself clear?"

They all nodded their heads and said, "Yes."

Paul looked down at Spider and said, "Your brother will be getting a visit tonight just to make sure the message is clear."

Paul started walking back to his motorcycle, then turned to Spider and said, "You owe Johnny a new pair of sneakers. Size 10, Johnny?" Paul asked.

John smiled and said, "Yes."

Paul got back on his motorcycle and raised his hand in a circular motion.

The biker at the far end of the alley came roaring down while Paul and the Bull started their motorcycles.

They all roared away as quickly as they came.

The gang of thugs was left stunned, and Spider worried what would happen to his brother.

The bikers rode back to Mr. Billing's hardware store to drop John off.

As the Bull stood up on his motorcycle, John got off. The bull noticed John's cell phone on his belt.

He asked to see it. The Bull typed in "Guardian Angles" and a phone number, then handed the phone back to John.

He smiled and said, "If you ever have any problems with anyone, just call this number, and we'll be back." He finally took off his glasses. "Just use it wisely."

They all stayed to watch John walk back into the hardware store.

Then they roared down the street on their motorcycles.

Inside the store, Mr. Billings asked how his lunch was.

John just laughed and said, "It was great."

That night, after work, still bewildered by the day's events, John opened the back gate of Sitto's garden.

He found Sitto sitting under the trellis, full of grapes.

She was cleaning and sorting tomatoes.

He sat down beside her and grabbed a handful of grapes, while she rubbed the dirt off the tomatoes.

From a distance, they heard the 6:00 p.m. bells of Saint Stephen's Church.

Sitto looked at John and smiled as she listened to the rhythm of church bells.

That night in the house of correction, Joe Collins was stirring a pot of boiling water in the prison kitchen. He turned to see a very large biker standing behind him.

The biker stared at Joe and said, "Your brother thinks he can retaliate against the people who put you here."

"See to it that it doesn't happen again. Don't make me have to come back here."

A few days later, at John's basketball practice, his coach handed him a box with a new pair of basketball shoes.

He said, "Someone dropped them off for you and left in a big hurry."

John never saw Spider again and never told his friend Billy what had happened.

The End

# About the Author

Fate loves the fearless.

—James Russell Lowell

Fate has brought the author down several interesting paths in life that he would like to share—from nostalgic moments growing up in his city of Worcester, Massachusetts, through his working life.

The author reminisces about many lighthearted true stories from his past intertwined with a variety of short stories based on real people.